SHORT SHORTS

Childhood Stories for Grown-up Kids

Jennifer Jamieson Woods

SHORT SHORTS

Published in the
United States of America by the
Independent Writers Studio Press
in Bellingham, Washington

ISBN: 978-1-7341878-8-5
Sketches of Jennifer by Eva Prager.
Author photo and Small, the Bear photo
by Christine Griffin.

Book Design by Mary Elizabeth Gillilan.

Dedication

This book is dedicated to my family (in order of age) Liz, Wendy, Tom, Candy, David and of course my mum, who never let me forget that I was the youngest of us all.

Three of us have passed and three of us remain.

Rest in Peace,
Mum (Frieda LaPlante Jamieson Carmichal)
Liz (Dr Elizabeth Jamieson Prockop Rusche)
David (David Colin Jamieson),
Tom (Thomas Northy Jamieson)

Contents

Jennifer, at the age of two, sketched by Eva Prager, the renowned Canadian artist, after seeing Jennifer at play on the beach. 1954.

Cape Cod

"Come get your suitcases," Mum called from the attic, handing out the bags to my siblings. I didn't know what she was talking about, but I felt relief when she told my oldest sister, "Lynn, you help Jennifer get her things together." I was two and a half and didn't have a clue as to what was going on. "Remember, we will be gone for five days—that means five underpants, at least three t-shirts, pants, shorts, socks, and pajamas. Bring your swimsuits and runners, too. We'll probably all wear our sandals."

Lynn took me into my bedroom, and we began to pack. "Mum," Lynn called, "Jennifer doesn't have a swimsuit."

"Carrie probably has one she can wear," our mother replied.

Lynn disappeared for a while and came back with a red swimsuit. She held it up to me and said, "It might be a bit big, but it will do."

I had only been wading in the lake in my shorts; I never had a swimsuit. I was curious where we were going. "Hugger bear?" I held him out to her.

"Sure, you can bring him along. We are going to the ocean," Lynn said. "Cape Cod."

I didn't have the whole story, but Lynn told me that Dad

had been born and raised in an outport on the east coast of Newfoundland. He told Lynn the sea ran in his blood. He needed to be on the ocean.

Early the next morning, our suitcases and a picnic basket, which I hoped was full of food, went into the trunk of the car.

My four older siblings sat in the back. In the front, I sat next to Mum, and my brother, Phil, sat next to our dad.

The drive went on forever. We stopped for bathroom breaks and a meal. I had my hugger bear with me, and he and I had grand conversations. I made his voice high and squeaky. Mum finally said, "Stop that squeaking, or I'll take him away from you." It wasn't easy sitting still. It was uncomfortable. My mother yelled, "Jennifer, just quit your wiggling."

Mum and my oldest sister smoked, and the car was getting so stuffy. "Window, please?" I asked.

"Not my window," said Mum, "It will mess my hair."

"All right, I'll open mine," said my brother, Tim. "You baby."

Phil fell asleep, and I did, too. It was a relief.

We finally arrived at the seaside. Our cottage was right across the street from the ocean. We all ran to get in the water. After an eight-hour drive, we were happy to be out of the car.

"Hey, the water tastes like salt," Tim called.

I had only waded to my knees but put my hand in to taste the water. It did taste like salt, but not like the salt we put on our food. I didn't like it. I had only been in freshwater before.

Each day, we played at the beach. We made sandcastles, buried each other in sand, and collected shells and sea glass. My older siblings swam, but I only waded. I enjoyed the tide pools with all the little creatures in them. Sometimes, there were tiny crabs, minnows, and shells. Mum sat in a chair with a straw hat on her head. She read her book and kept an eye on us.

While playing on the beach one afternoon, a woman approached Mum. She had a large pad of paper and a tin box. "Excuse me," she said.

"Yes," Mum replied.

The woman pointed at me and asked, "Is this your daughter?"

"Yes, she's my youngest."

"How many children do you have?"

"Six."

"Oh my," the woman said.

She introduced herself as Eva Prager, an artist whose work my mother knew. "I would like to do some drawings of your little girl. She's so darling."

"Not now. She's having fun. I want to let her play," Mum said.

"Can I come by after dinner?" Eva asked.

"I suppose, what time?"

"Seven?"

"That would be fine."

After dinner, Lynn brushed out my hair and dressed me in clean clothes. Eva Prager arrived and very quickly drew several sketches of me. She featured hugger-bear in one. She used crayons as her drawing tools. The artist gave Mum a choice of four drawings.

The following day, Mum had us dress with our swimsuits underneath our clothes. She brought a picnic basket full of food. We drove down to the marina with all eight of us in the car. We walked along the dock until we came to a sailboat more than twice our car's size. Mum made Phil and me wear a life vest.

Once we had settled in the boat, Dad turned on the motor and took us out into the bay. He then shut off the engine and directed my brother to hoist the sails. The quiet of sailing and the gentle rocking of the boat gave me pleasure. We anchored near the shore to have dinner. Mum served lobster with nutcrackers and picks, a yucky-looking dinner to me, so she gave me a precooked hot dog with lots of ketchup.

When I finished eating, Mum told Lynn, "Take Jennifer up front and get her ready for bed."

We were going to spend the night on the boat. I was excited.

I sat with Lynn as we looked out the round window. "Look at the sea," she said. "It goes on forever."

As I peered out the window, I tried to imagine what forever would be like.

Jennifer, at the age of two, sketched by Eva Prager. 1954.

Three Little Kids

We were just three little kids: my sister, Carrie, my brother, Phil, and me, out for a ride in the back seat of our mother's fancy new tan-colored Cadillac Coupe de Ville. It was a large roomy car with a scent that emanated from the leather interior. Since this was in the 1950s, there were no seatbelts, and we roamed, unfettered and free, in the immense regions of the back seat. Carrie, at age seven, was the oldest of the three of us. She could stand on the floor and look over the seat to the front where the chrome dashboard loomed, and the window looked out onto the road ahead. Despite being a small five-year-old, Phil could stand on the driveline hump and look out over the seat. As a petite three-year-old, the only way that I could see to the front was to stand on the back seat.

As children will do, naturally, my brother and sister joined me once I stood on the back seat. Soon we were jumping up and down and screaming with glee as Mum drove on; we were going shopping.

She looked in the rearview mirror and cautioned, "Sit down! Your feet don't belong on those new leather seats!" We were having too much fun to comply with such a wimpy directive. Before long, her voice was raised to a louder tone,

"Sit down, and I mean it. All of you just sit down!" Still, our mirth and joy were not to be inhibited, even by her angry tone of voice. She then turned towards the back seat; her left hand remained on the wheel while her right hand reached back and swatted towards us. We pinned ourselves against the back seat, laughing as her hand ineffectually batted the air. Oh, the thrill of being naughty and getting away with it!

Now, Mum was a proud woman, and this was her brand-new Cadillac. We were out to run errands around our hometown of Niagara Falls. She was the wife of a prominent doctor, known to many people, and having a back seat full of out-of-control children, no doubt, was not her idea of dignity.

She yelled angrily, "You'll be sorry when we get home." She then cut our outing short, turned the car around, and took us straight home.

Yes, we were sorry when we got home. We all had to stand side-by-side in the kitchen, bare-bottomed and contrite, whimpering our regrets in as many ways as we could think. We cried in anticipation of what might happen next. Mum went to the skinny drawer in the kitchen, which held the knives. She pulled out a long gray strap. I had never seen this strap before, although I had heard of its existence. Our oldest brother, Tim, had told of how he had been struck by the strap for his numerous infractions. I watched as she took the long rigid strap and began her punishment regime. She went down the line of our trio, starting with Carrie, then Phil; she saved me for last.

Whap, whap, whap on each of our little bare bottoms went the strap. The sting was sharp and raw.

"Now go outside and play," she commanded as she put the strap back into the drawer. We covered our bottoms and followed orders.

Later that night, as we prepared for our communal bath, bottoms bare once more, we compared our strap welts before getting into the tub. When I lowered myself into the water, my wounded bottom stung, but I remembered my mirth in the back seat of Mum's brand new Cadillac.

Frog Tales

Up to our thighs in the murky water, we swished around the pond. My sister, Carrie, and I could not keep away. Our understanding neighbors didn't care if we spent all day out there. We did no harm.

The pond was no bigger than our living room. A large weeping willow hung over it; the leaves almost touched the water. Cattails lined a portion of the shore while the neighbor's lawn came down to the third side. We could easily be absorbed for hours as we searched and observed the life of the pond.

Water skeeters glided across the surface, making light ripples as they moved. The frogs were a good handful in size and were easy to catch. I felt great glee as I captured one and felt its slimy body squirm in my hands. I could feel its fingers dig into my skin, and its feet push off. There were no nails at the end of their digits. Eventually, it would be still. Maybe it perceived that I meant it no ill as I held it in my five-year-old hands. I remember petting their heads and singing, "Five green and speckled frogs." I liked to believe that my tenderness towards them helped them feel safe.

Once, I found a pair of frogs stuck together early in the spring and was about to separate them when Carrie screamed at me, "Leave them alone." I knew by the tone of her voice that I needed to comply. Then the jelly mass appeared: opaque white, with black dots throughout. I wondered what that could be. I got yelled at once again when I put my hand into the murky white glob to feel it. My brief touch revealed a thick but yielding batch of goo that felt soft, like a nearly set gelatin. I could not feel any lumps that might be the black stipples.

Each time we visited the pond, I would swish over to the area where the dotted profusion was situated, until one day I could see wiggling within it. I noticed that the dots had slight tails twitching within the cloudy clump of jelly. "Look," I blurted to Carrie, "they're moving."

"Yeah," she responded, "they're going to be tadpoles."

"When do you think that'll be?" I was curious.

"Sometime soon," she answered.

I imagined the tailed dots breaking free of the mass and swimming off. They seemed so tiny.

The next time we went to the pond, the white glob was gone. Had they become tadpoles so quickly? Where were they? I looked down into the water and saw the tadpoles swimming everywhere, propelled by their new tails. I picked one up only briefly, somehow knowing they were in a sensitive state. Its eye seemed large in comparison to its body. The little tail flicked in my hand. I returned it to the water in haste, knowing that air was not its medium for breath. I stood calmly and waited until the murkiness settled and I could see. As the water cleared, the tadpoles swarmed around my ankles. I thought I felt light nibbles. I could've stood there forever as the tiny creatures gathered around me. Dinner came far too early for me that night.

The next morning, I was eager to return to the pond. I was not allowed to go by myself. I had to have Carrie with me. Finally, after a long wait, she said, "Oh, alright. Let's go."

I ran to the pond but stopped at the shore to step carefully in the mud so as to stir up as little of the murkiness as I could. Again, I stood motionless as I allowed the water to become transparent. There they were, those tiny tadpoles with their tails flipping back and forth to propel them. Did they look bigger today? It seemed possible.

I was not free to go to the pond for the next two days. We had family business to take care of. I thought about the tadpoles the whole time, champing at the bit to get back to the pond.

"Can we go to the pond today?" I asked Carrie.

"It's only morning; we haven't even had breakfast. Later maybe."

I hated being at the whim of an older sibling. Mum never let me do anything by myself except sit in my room.

Finally, Carrie said, "OK, let's go to the pond." I ran ahead of her as she followed me.

In the water, I shuffled along so as not to ruffle the soft pond's bottom. There they were! The little tadpoles swam all around. They were about twice the size as they had been two days prior. Their dark charcoal color stood out in the water like currants in rice pudding.

Weeks went by until one day, the tadpoles had hind legs. They no longer needed their tails for travel; their legs did the job now. What would happen to their tails? Would they fall off?

One morning, upon arriving at the pond, we saw a muskrat disappear into the cattails with a frog in its mouth, kicking furiously. I ran around the pond trying to rescue the frog, but the muskrat had slipped away. The poor frogs were so vulnerable. I had not known that they were fodder for other animals. I knew that big birds such as herons ate frogs, but there were no herons where we lived. I had thought the frogs were safe from predators in this small pond.

The legs of the young frogs developed muscles as the tail disappeared. Where did they go? I wanted to find a tail floating in the water. I would've loved to have examined it.

After the back legs of the frogs got stronger, the tiny front legs appeared magically. It seemed like they grew up overnight. Now the little frogs swam like adults. They looked tiny as they propelled their bodies forward with their new legs. I loved watching them as they swam in the water. I picked one up, and it wriggled in my hand. I quickly replaced it, careful not to damage it.

I totally neglected the big frogs as I witnessed the tadpoles grow and change. I could still find some along the shore, but there did not seem to be so many as there had been.

* * *

Mum announced that Dad was coming for a visit—I had to take a bath, wash my hair, and wear my seersucker outfit. When Dad arrived, he came in the back door through the garage as if he lived there. He kissed each one of us on the cheek. All six of us sat in the living room. Phil and I sat on the floor.

My oldest sister, Lynn, sat on the couch next to Dad. Mum went into the kitchen. During his visit, he primarily spoke with my two older sisters. He couldn't ask about school since it was the summer. When it came time for him to speak to me, he asked, "So, Jennifer, what have you been doing?"

"I've been watching tadpoles grow into frogs. Did you know that they still have their tails when their back legs grow in?" My voice was high with excitement.

"Yes, I do know that," he answered as he turned again towards Lynn.

I couldn't see why the visit from Dad was such a big deal and why Mum left the room. As I sat on the floor in my itchy seersucker outfit, I thought about the frogs.

When Dad left, we all sat down to dinner; the conversation focused on his visit. Lynn said that he looked good.

He did? I hadn't noticed anything different about him. Mum remained quiet during the whole meal.

After dinner, Phil and I did the dishes. He washed, and I dried. My oldest brother put the dishes away in the cupboards since I couldn't reach, and Mum didn't want me to stand on a chair.

The next day, Carrie and I went to the pond right after breakfast. I tiptoed onto the muddy bottom and quietly got to the place where the frogs hung out."Where did all the frogs go?"

"It looks like there was a raccoon here last night." Carrie pointed at the mud on the shore.

"How do you know that?"

"See those footprints? They're raccoons."

"Raccoons!" I squealed. "They eat frogs?"

"Sorry, sis, they do,"

"Oh, no, all my little frogs got eaten," I cried.

"Not all of them; there are still a few left." She tried to soften the blow.

"But there were at least a hundred of them—now, I only see about ten or so."

"Yes, it's a harsh reality. Animals have to eat."

"My poor little frogs," I whimpered.

We stayed at the pond for a little while, but I felt sad about the frogs, so we went home.

That night when Mum tucked me into bed, I cried as I told her about my frogs getting eaten by raccoons.

"That is a sad part of life. It happens," she said.

"Like Dad's not living with us anymore?" I asked. "That's sad, too."

"Yes, it is," said Mum.

Sweet Cherry Border

We ran freely that summer—the summer my parents got divorced. My mother moved us from Niagara Falls to Oakville, Ontario, to a house with lots of trees. I was the youngest at five and a half. I was the baby. I tagged along behind my brother and my sister, Carrie, as we ran through the trees. Going home was for food and to go to the bathroom, although Phil was bold enough to "water a tree," as he called it.

Our next-door neighbors were an elderly couple who had raised their family and were happy to have children running around once more. I remember the woman was especially sweet to me. She enjoyed watching us explore the pond in their backyard. An old weeping willow hung over the pond; its water was a murky, soft-bottomed mud, while the surface was alive with water skeeters, frogs, dragonflies, and vegetation. There were few other pleasures greater than that mud between my toes and a frog in my hands. It was a haven for the three of us. All we had to do was find a hole in the hedge that bordered our properties, knock on the neighbor's door, say hello, and we were in frog heaven.

School started, and we had to return to living with shoes on our feet and starchy uniforms. It was a harsh adjustment after a summer of wild abandon. But the pond was always there when we got home after school. In the winter, it froze solid, and I worried about my frog friends stuck in the ice. "They're alright," my neighbor sweetly said, "they always come back every year."

The spring brought a wonder I had never seen before. The entire hedge bloomed full and pink with little tiny flowers that had a faint fruity fragrance. The whole hedge was abuzz with bees flitting from tiny flower to tiny flower. When I asked the neighbor why the hedge was so full of blossoms, she said, "Why, honey, that's a Japanese cherry bush."

"Japanese cherry," I had never heard of such a thing. "Are there actually cherries?'

"Yes, honey, at the end of July that hedge will be full of cherries."

"Full of cherries," I repeated.

"But you can't eat them."

"Can't eat them? Why not?"

"They're bitter—they're bird food!"

"Bird food?" I couldn't believe it.

Meanwhile, the pond was full of adventure. After spending time stuck together, the frogs had produced masses of black-eyed jelly. Phil told me they were frog eggs and to keep an eye on them.

This was the perfect job for me. Every day that I could, I would find my way through the hedge of flowers to look at the frog eggs. Just as the flowers fell from the hedge, the tadpoles sprouted from the mass of jelly. There were hundreds of them. I loved watching them swim around in a container full of water that I scooped out of the pond. The water was too cold to wade in, and I had no rubber boots.

When the tadpoles sprouted their back legs, the flowers were gone from the hedge. By the time the tadpoles had four legs, the hedge was growing little round cherries. The summer was with us, and we were now running barefoot again, wading in the pond, and enjoying our freedom.

The tadpoles lost their round heads as their tails disappeared, and became full-fledged frogs. Each one was dear to me as I picked them up and examined it. The vulnerability of these little fragile lives was evident to me because I had played a part in their growth with my vigilant, watchful eye.

If I hadn't passed through the hedge daily, I might have missed the other natural wonder that was happening. The cherries ripened. They were not yet soft, but they were starting to turn red. Unlike domestic cherries, they did not have a long stem but clung to the end of the branches and between the leaves.

One day, I couldn't resist. I plucked a cherry off the bush and popped it in my mouth. It didn't stay in my mouth for long. The hard bitter flavor of it gagged me. My disappointment was deep. I had so wanted them to taste good.

The following week, I spent most days at the pond. The weather had turned hot and humid; the pond was a relief. When I was in the pond playing catch and release with "my" frogs, Carrie found me. She held out her hand to me, saying, "Try one! They're delicious."

I saw that she had a few of the Japanese cherries. "No thanks, they're too bitter for me."

"But they're not," she persisted, "try one."

I took a cherry from her hand—it felt softer than the one I had tried before. I popped it into my mouth, and she was right. I could still taste the bitterness, but the dominant flavor was sweet and warm.

"Mmm," I said to her, "it's warm."

"That's from the sun," Carrie said, "I think that's also why they're so sweet."

Leaving the cool of the pond, I ran through the hedge to our side of the property, not wanting our neighbor to see me.

I found a patch of berries and began eating. The pits inside were small and went far with a good strong spit. My sister and I ate our fill of them, and then we went home.

In less than an hour, my stomach was churning and turning full of cherries. I went to bed without any supper. The next morning, I had diarrhea. I ate a bowl of cereal and went out to play.

Being drawn to the cherries, I went back to the bush. Again, I ate the delicious little fruit to the point of sickness. I couldn't seem to resist. The results the next day were the same.

This went on for a week or so, and then the cherries began to drop off the bush. My feeding frenzy was over, and my stomach returned to normal.

Each summer for the next three years, I suffered through the dreariness of school, waiting for spring so I could watch over the pond life and feast on the Japanese cherries. I never learned the lesson of restraint. I couldn't help myself. They were so delicious. My neighbor never caught us eating the berries, and I don't know what she would've said if she had. Never again in my life have I encountered a Japanese cherry bush.

Those summers remain in my memory where the sweet gave me pain, but I made no path to resistance. I don't doubt that if I were to find a ripe Japanese cherry bush in fruit again, I would gorge myself until the pain was intolerable, and only then would I walk away.

The Jockey

"You can see his eyes." Carrie points to the hatch in the attic that is in our bedroom closet. It is propped open a few inches. "He's looking at us right now."

I peer up. I can see something, but I'm not sure it's eyes. "I can't really see anything."

"He's wearing a mask," my sister says.

"A mask?"

"So the mud from the track doesn't get in his eyes."

"The track?" I don't know what she is talking about.

"He's a jockey. He's hiding out here. He's got some bad debts. He stays in the attic all day and only comes out at night, while we are asleep," she adds.

"He comes out at night?"

"Yeah, he comes down from up there in our closet, and then he walks around the house. He goes to the kitchen to eat."

My skin prickles at the thought of this jockey wandering around in our house at night and eating our food. "But why does a jockey stay here?"

"There's a track near Toronto."

Toronto is close by—it's a possibility.

"What are debts?" I ask, in my six-year-old innocence.

"Bets he has lost. People bet big money on horse races."

I know about bets. My big brother is always betting us for candy, food, or sometimes money. "I bet you ten cents I can put this whole potato chip into my mouth without breaking it," I've heard Tim say. My sister lost the bet as he deftly eased the mammoth chip into his mouth without breaking it. As far as I can tell, he never loses a bet. I guess the jockey is not so lucky.

At night, before I go to bed, I always make certain that the cupboard door is closed. Then I lie in bed and watch, waiting to see him come out of the closet. Even though my apprehension is great, I always seem to fall asleep before his appearance. I look for evidence of him in our room and throughout the house every day.

In the cacophonous chaos of breakfast, with the six of us kids and Mum in the kitchen that barely accommodates our dinner table, we rush to get food to eat and find our lunches. "I swear someone comes in and eats our food at night," says Mum. "I baked at least two dozen cookies last night, and they are half gone. The milk is almost gone, too." Carrie and I make eye contact across the room. The jockey was here last night.

One night when I was up to use the bathroom, I swear I saw a shadow disappear down the stairs. The jockey.

Another time, I woke up in the morning to find the closet door open when I was certain that I had closed it the night before.

My sleep becomes fitful as I worry about the presence of the jockey in our house at night. One night at dinner, I fall asleep with a forkful of potatoes in my hand. "What's the matter with you?"Mum asks.

"I guess I'm just tired."

"Well, why don't you go to your room and go to sleep right now?" Mum commands.

Oh no, in my room without Carrie. Would the jockey know that?

I go upstairs. It is still light out, and I believe the jockey doesn't come out until dark. I make certain the closet door is closed, nonetheless.

Someone comes to our room when I'm in early twilight sleep, and I wake with a startle and scream.

"What are you screaming about?" Carrie asks. "It's just me!"

"I thought you were the jockey."

"You'll never see him. He's really sly," she says.

"Have you seen him?" I ask.

"I saw his leg when he crawled back into the hatch one time. He had on white skinny pants. He didn't look very big."

"You saw him?"

"Yup," she replies.

"Did he see you?"

"I doubt it, but he knows we are here."

I pull myself in tight, feeling vulnerable.

***

"The jockey!" my husband says. 'We have to close the closet because of the jockey? What jockey?"

I tell him the story of how my childhood nights were haunted by the jockey who lived in the attic and how he came out at night and wandered through the house and ate our food.

"I must admit that does sound scary," he validates me. "Surely, you don't believe in the jockey anymore."

"No, not really, but there is a hatch in our closet." Together we peer into our wardrobe. Up in the ceiling is the hatch to the attic. Mercifully, it is fully closed.

I no longer believe in the jockey in the attic, but I do always make certain that the closet door is closed at night before I go to bed. Just in case.

Sister Bertrand

She was huge compared to my five-year-old self. Her body, clad mostly in black, towered over all of us first graders at St. Mary's Catholic School. Her long veil fell past her waist and was anchored around her head by a stiff, starchy fabric, white as white, never a smudge or a spot. The white framed her face and pushed the flesh of her forehead down a bit, her jowls forward, and her jaw line up. This made her look as if she had forced her head into a tube or a very tight turtle neck. As a result of this face-squishing, there was much jiggling and wiggling of her flesh as she spoke. Her wiggling flesh seemed to be a millisecond behind the rest of her face. Then it took another millisecond to flap back into place. It was as if her flesh was an echo of her face, a mini-time warp—word, paused delay then wiggle of flesh. Stop. Then, word, paused delay and wiggle of flesh. Mum was a thin, fine-boned woman; there was no visible jiggling flesh on her body.

As a five-year-old, sometimes I was mesmerized by Sister Bertrand's jiggling jowls and heard nothing she said. "Jennifer!" She raised her voice, making her flesh move in sync with her sharp, quick, and harsh tone. She had my attention.

"What was I just saying?"

I had no clue what she had been talking about. My attention was brought to the auditory realm only because she said my name. Before that, I was all eyes, enthralled by the dance of her jowls. Quickly, I came to a sense of reality, "Jesus?" I asked. It was worth a try, wasn't this Catholic school?

"No, you foolish little girl, I was talking about recess."

Then I opened my mouth to say a few words that would mark the beginning of my lifelong struggle with the nuns who were my teachers. "It kind of rhymes, doesn't it? Jesus, recess?"

"Why, you impudent little…" In a flash, she was in front of me, the flesh of her double chin waggled before me. I looked up at her, and whaaap, she slapped me across the face before I could say anything in response. Now, this was not the first time someone had slapped me in the face, but this was the first time I felt my neck twist far enough to align my chin with my shoulder. I felt the blood in my cheek rise with humiliation as my classmates gaped at me in utter silence.

"Let that be a lesson to you all," said Sister Bertrand, waggling her index finger at our class. "There will be no smart talk in this classroom. Do you hear me?" Silently, everyone nodded in conformity to this edict.

SMALL

He was two and a half inches tall, covered in soft mohair. His eyes were dark beads; his mouth sewn in a permanent smirk. His shoulders, hips, and neck were articulated. I was six years old when I received him as a birthday gift. As soon as I looked into his beady little eyes, it was love. I called my new little teddy bear Small because that's what he was.

He was perfectly sized to fit inside my hand, with his head sticking out above my fingers. Small fit into my jeans pocket, and into the pocket of the dress coat that I wore to Sunday Mass. And best of all, he fit into the pocket of my school uniform without any part of him showing. I always found it a comfort to reach in and feel his furry little body.

At home, when he was in my jeans pocket, he joined in our play. He would poke his head out to look at how high I had climbed a tree. The little bear had his own chair at tea parties, and he sat on my lap as I swung back and forth on the swing. He even rode on the handlebars of my tricycle. My mother would not let him sit on the table for meals, but I could keep him on my lap as long as he stayed out of trouble.

At church, I could reach my hand into my pocket and feel him waiting for me. I always made certain he was in the pocket on the side away from my mother. He was a comfort when Mass seemed to be endlessly long, or the priest jumbled on in Latin.

Small was a special comfort at school as I struggled to learn to write both letters and numbers. I would reach into my pocket to feel his presence while my classmates zipped through their writing, and I grappled with the daunting task of putting pencil to paper. Nonetheless, I was sure he smiled as I read aloud to my teacher and my classmates.

Then one day, Sister Bertrand said to me, "Jennifer, what are you playing with?"

"Nothing," I said in return.

There she was, by my side. "Put it in my hand." I looked at her upturned palm.

I hesitated and hesitated and then pulled Small out of my pocket. I looked into his eyes before I placed him in her hand, uncertain if I would ever see him again.

She held him up in front of the class and said, "Look what Jennifer had in her pocket."

All my classmates laughed.

She then took Small and put him into her desk drawer.

At the end of the school day, I asked Sister Bertrand, "Can I have my little bear back?"

"Will I ever see him at school again?"

"No, Sister," I answered.

"Very well then …" and she opened her desk drawer, got him out, and put him into my outstretched hand.

When I dressed for school the next day, I longed to put Small into my pocket. He sat on my dresser and looked at me with his dark eyes. I grabbed him and put him into my pocket, and stuffed a hanky over the top of him.

I tried my best to keep my hand out of my pocket, but then we had a spelling test. I needed comfort. I could spell just fine, but Sister Bertrand did not offer us enough time in between for me to get the words written in full. I needed to print slowly to make my letters readable. As I wrote, I reached my left hand for Small, who was in my right pocket.

Sister Bertrand was at my side. "Give it to me," she said.

I reached into my pocket and got out my little bear. Whap she slapped me across the face.

"I told you never to bring that thing back to school, yet here it is." She held my little teddy bear up for my classmates to laugh at again.

I sat at my desk, hands in my lap, tears streaming, with no solace to turn to.

After the school day, I asked Sister Bertrand if I could have my teddy bear back.

"I'm calling your mother," she said. She did not open her desk drawer.

My lap sat empty as we ate our dinner. That night Mum said she needed to talk to me. She recounted the whole story of how Small was in my pocket at school, the way Sister Bertrand had recited it to her. "Why did you take him to school, Jennifer?" she asked.

"He's my friend."

"Don't you have other friends at school?"

"Not like Small."

"No, I suppose not. He's pretty special, isn't he?"

"Yes, he makes me feel good."

Mum and I visited my classroom after school the next day. "I would like my daughter's small bear back, please." My mother and Sister Bertrand were about the same height, only my mother was slender.

Sister Bertrand went to her desk and opened the drawer, got out my bear, and put him into Mum's outstretched hand. She turned and gave him to me. I hugged Small to my face. I had missed him.

In the car on the way home, Mum said, "Now, Jennifer, you can't take Small to school with you. Sister Bertrand may just take him away from you forever."

"Take him away from me. No!" I exclaimed.

"I wouldn't put it past her. You better keep him at home, or you could lose him forever," Mum said. "She's that kind of person."

I held Small up close to my mouth, "Well, buddy, I guess you'll have to stay home while I go to school."

"He'll be fine," Mum said.

The next day, I left Small on my dresser and went to school. Numerous times, I reached into my pocket only to find nothing there.

When I got home, I ran to my room to see Small. There he sat on my dresser in a tiny rocking chair. Mum came in my room and said, "I thought he was missing you, so I got him a chair to sit in while he waits for you to come home."

Each day at school, I would feel a little warm spot in my heart as I pictured Small sitting in his rocking chair waiting for me.

***

Small is in my life today. He's in his early sixties, and he looks a little worse for wear. One ear is essentially gone, and his lower face is shredded. I got there just in time, as one of my dogs was about to devour him. I dare not move his legs or arms for fear they would fall off. His eyes remain the sparkling beads as they were when I first laid my eyes on him. And my dear little Small still sits in his rocking chair as he waits for me to come home to my desk.

Small waiting patiently, as little bears do, for Jennifer.

Morning Oatmeal

The summer cottage was a welcome reprieve from our home in Niagara Falls. I felt so many restrictions at our big English Tudor house. One in particular that I never understood was "don't touch the walls." What was that about? Why couldn't we touch the walls?

At the cottage, we had plenty of touchable things. One of my favorites was a toy owl whose wings were on a string and would flap when I pulled it. I listened to music I had never heard before on an old turntable that played 78 rpm records.

Up a steep staircase at the cottage was one big room where all six of us kids slept in bunk beds along the walls. The bathroom was outside; I hated the outhouse. I didn't like to touch any part of it, but we had to. It stank and was dark even in the daylight. I had seen a huge spider in there one time and screamed and screamed until my mother came running. "It's only a spider, Jennifer," Mum said.

"But it's huge," I screamed.

"Alright, come inside." She led me to the cottage. There was a bathroom inside that I never knew existed. It was adjacent to the downstairs room where Mum slept. Why didn't I know about this indoor bathroom?

At the cottage, we spent most of our time outside. There was so much to do. The lake was right in our front yard with a dock and a small boat. The soft sand of the shore gave my brother, Phil, and me many hours as young naturalists catching crayfish, minnows, frogs, and even an occasional snake. We spent the entire time in our bathing suits. We got terrible sunburns. Phil would get fat blisters on his shoulders that looked like they hurt, but he never complained.

I loved the boat. It had two seats and two oars. Mum allowed me to row to the end of an extended rope and back again all by myself, provided I had a life jacket on. I never tired of the back and forth of my maneuvers. I could see some other cottages along the shore at the end of the rope and then the cottage's buildings as I rowed to shore.

The buildings on our property included the house itself, the outhouse, and a separate wash house where my mother did the laundry.

There was a ramshackle building that looked like a garage to me, but it was full of stuff like old furniture, barrels of who knows what, rope, hoses, what I thought were car parts, and many cardboard boxes in various states of dilapidation. It had no room for Mother's car. She parked alongside the cottage. She never took the car anywhere except to buy groceries. She would always go by herself and return with the many bags of food needed to feed our six mouths. My oldest sister was left behind to keep the rest of us in line.

Maybe, once a week, Mum gave my big sister, Lynn, a handful of change. I knew that meant a visit to the candy store. We walked to the store in a single file along the side of the road. We lined up according to our ages: Lynn led us, and I trailed at the end as the youngest. Phil and I would play chase or shadow tag and fall out of step. Lynn would yell at us, "Get off the road." We would do as she said.

The candy store had more than candy, but that was all I saw. At eye level, there were two shelves of bins all full of candy. There were jelly beans, cinnamon candies, root beer barrels, hard-shelled chocolate candies, and others that I could not name. Lynn would give each of us two pennies. Ever the smart one, my sister Carrie would get black balls since they were three for a penny. She had six candies to savor the rest of the day.

Phil would choose root beer barrels, which were a penny each. I chose one stick of red raspberry licorice for two cents. None of the other candies interested me. I could make my length of licorice last for a long time, but not, of course, as long as Carrie's black balls. Still, I was satisfied with my choice.

The big moment came when Lynn put the nickel into the gumball machine. They were bigger than a cherry and came in a rainbow of colors. We all stood in anticipation to see what color came rolling down the chute. It didn't matter what color we got because it was a rare event for us to chew gum. Mum thought that gum chewing was a disgusting habit.

As we walked back to the cottage, each of us enjoyed our special treat. Lynn held on to the gumball.

When we arrived back at the cottage, Lynn handed over the gumball to Mum. We all stood and watched as she carefully cut it into six pieces. She then handed out our share of the treat. "Now, outside, all of you," she said. I thought she sent us outdoors so she didn't have to watch us chew. I could only chew the gum for a short period of time, and then it would be gone. I must have swallowed it.

Each morning at the cottage, Mum would shoo us outside to go swimming while she made oatmeal. I asked her why we had to go swimming first. She told me that the oatmeal would taste much better after our swim.

Swimming was fun. As a diminutive five-year-old, I couldn't swim yet and only waded out to waist-high in the water. My older brother, Tim, would pick me up and toss me into the water, both a thrill and a terror as I struggled to find my feet. Lynn and Beth, would have me swim back and forth between them. Of course, I used the dog paddle and could barely keep my head above the water. Tim jumped off the dock. None of the others tried that. I remember Phil and I would test each other to see how long we could stay underwater. Whenever Carrie joined in this game, we all opened our eyes under the clear water and waved at each other.

Wet and chilly, we'd get out of the water and were delighted to see Mum as she came to shore to greet us with six towels. The shivers followed me all the way to the kitchen, where the oatmeal would be served. I remember sitting on a stool at the kitchen counter, a towel draped over my shoulders, my ponytail dripping down my back as I waited for my bowl of oatmeal.

I watched Mum ladle out the porridge. When it arrived steaming and fragrant, it always had a big dollop of butter melting in the middle. We were then allowed only two spoonfuls of brown sugar. Mother poured milk around the outside of the oatmeal, and I would stir it all up in anticipation of my first bite. Still shivering from my swim, I would fill my spoon and then my mouth with the warm and nourishing breakfast. It tasted delicious. Mum was right.

***

I never gave any thought to the fact that Dad was not with us. He had not been around much at home anyway. Lynn mentioned him only to be shushed by Mother. As an adult, I learned the reason Dad was not with us. He had another woman who was expecting his baby. Mum had chosen to take all of us away so that we did not have to witness his transgressions. This must have been the beginning of the dissolution of my parents' marriage.

The following summer, we moved away from Niagara Falls.

Cafeteria Catastrophe

Our young feet echoed on the stairs as we walked in a line down into the hall that led to the cafeteria at St. Mary's Catholic School in Oakville, Ontario. The old stone structure, built before the twentieth century, had two stories. The cafeteria and gym were in the basement, and classrooms were on the first floor. Our first-grade teacher, Sister Bertrand, had strict expectations that we adhered to whenever we traveled throughout the school. We were to walk quietly in a line, arms by our sides, eyes front. I was always behind Peter Banner and in front of Mary Flynn. Upon arriving in the cafeteria, we sat at our designated table.

At this time in my life, I was what could be called an extremely sensitive and squeamish eater. A small shell fragment in an egg salad sandwich made me gag. I left the room at the smell of liver and onions cooking. Sweet relish turned my stomach.

My school lunches mainly consisted of Kraft cheese between two slices of white bread lightly spread with Miracle Whip. I liked my sandwiches cut into little triangles, but I could not count on this since the lunch maker in our family was not always consistent. My older sisters enjoyed tormenting me, but had been given strict orders by my mother to make my sandwiches to my particular taste, but not necessarily cut to my preference. I was a scrawny little girl, and Mum wanted me to eat.

Peter Banner at my right ate everything from slimy-looking liverwurst, stinky pastrami, pickles, olives, and who knows what else. His entire lunch was overbearing. He also ate with great gusto, took large bites, and washed his food down with his milk while talking about hockey, which was his other passion besides food. Sometimes, I had to turn my body away from him and towards Mary Flynn to protect myself from his odoriferous feeding frenzy.

This day, in particular, he had wolfed down a sandwich of something I did not recognize, followed by celery sticks stuffed with a pink cream cheese dotted with red and green bits. He was just about to devour some chocolate chip cookies when he said in a rather loud voice, "I think I'm going to get sick." He then vomited the food he had consumed all over the table and into his lunchbox in front of him. Since the celery was the last to go in, it was logically the first to come up. It was all green and slimy and looked even worse than it had appeared when it was unchewed. The regurgitated sandwich was much worse. I could feel myself begin to heave. It was too much for me to bear; the smell was horrific, the sight ungodly. I began to vomit my lunch, which looked mild compared to his. The contents of my stomach returned to my lunch box and down the front of my gabardine uniform. The tips of my two braids dangled into the mix as well. I continued to heave even though my stomach was empty. Peter, beside me, was done and wiping his mouth with a napkin.

The cafeteria nun was all aflutter with rags, a garbage can, and reprimands. "What is going on over here? Couldn't you have raised your hands and gone to the bathroom?" To me in particular, she said, "Look at you, you're covered! I suppose we'll have to call your mother."

With this, I began to cry. "She's not home."

"What?" asked the cafeteria nun.

"She's not home." More tears rolled down my cheeks.

"How do you know she's not home?"

"She's at school," I answered.

"At school?"

"Yes, she goes to school—she's studying."

"Studying, what for?"

"I'm not sure." I couldn't use my napkin to wipe my tears since I vomited on it, so I let them flow.

"Well, I never.... What about your father?"

"My father?"

"Where is he?"

"In Niagara Falls."

"In Niagara Falls? What's he doing there?"

"He lives there." I was getting so uncomfortable with her questions that I felt sick again.

"He lives in Niagara Falls, your mother is in school, and you're covered in vomit, " the cafeteria nun was incredulous. "What will I do with you?"

All I could do was cry. I had no answer for this nun whose name I didn't know. I hoped she wouldn't get Sister Bertrand, who got mad at students if they sneezed. What would she do with me with vomit on my uniform? Finally, Mary Flynn said to me, "What about your sister?"

"What?"

"What about your sister, Carrie. Couldn't she help you out?"

I hadn't even thought about my sister, but she was right. Carrie would probably help me.

I reluctantly raised my hand, and the cafeteria nun said, "What is it now?"

"Can I have my sister, Carrie, she's in fourth grade, come and help me?"

"You mean pull her out of class just to clean up her sorry little sister who can't be polite enough to save her vomit for the bathroom?"

"Yes," I said.

"I have an idea. You go to the bathroom and clean yourself up. You're a big girl."

Mercifully, there was no one else in the bathroom. I looked at myself in the mirror. My face was pale; tears streamed down my cheeks. My braids were dotted with bits of regurgitated bread and cheese, as was the front of my uniform. I turned on the water as I leaned over the sink. There were two faucets, one for hot and one for cold, so I waited until I could gather enough water to splash my face. I could feel some of the distress of the whole incident wash away with each handful. I just kept going. Water ran down my elbows onto the floor. I didn't care. It felt so good to wash away the tears, the vomit, and the snot.

"What happened to you?" I recognized Carrie's voice. I turned off the water, and she held out a handful of paper towels when I looked up. "Here," she said, "dry off your face, and we'll see what we can do about your hair and your uniform."

I wiped off my face and arms and stared at the front of my uniform.

Carrie took my braids and said, "Bend over." Then she rinsed them off in the sink. She then took some wet paper towels and cleaned off the front of my uniform. With some hesitation, I asked her, "Carrie, what's Mum studying in school?"

"She's going to be a teacher?'

"A teacher!" My eyes widened as water dripped off my chin.

"Yeah, didn't you know that?"

"No, I didn't," I said. "Why is she going to be a teacher?"

"So she can get a job." Carrie kept rinsing out my braids.

"Why does she need a job?'

"To support us."

"Why does she need to support us?"

"Because Dad isn't going to?'

"He's not?"

"No, he's not?" Carrie went on. "Don't you know anything, Jennifer? Mum and Dad are split. He's gone."

"That's why he lives in Niagara Falls, and we live here?" I asked.

"Wow, you really don't know anything, do you?"

"Why did they split up?'

Carrie was silent for a while. Then she looked at me, straightened my collar, and said, "I think you can go back to your class now. I'll see you on the bus after school."

"Carrie," I said

"What?"

"Thanks for the help."

My Best Black Eye Ever

To Canadians, hockey is a sacred sport. The whole nation is glued to their TV sets to watch *Hockey Night* in Canada. The Olympic Gold medal is worn on the chest of each and every citizen. Everyone knows someone who has played "big time" hockey and is proud to tell the tale. The long summer months are but an interruption in the hockey season, as we wait on tenterhooks for it to freeze long enough to create the outdoor rink.

Even as a young girl in the late fifties and early sixties, I grew up with hockey fever. I knew the names of the big players; I knew the teams. I tried to get involved with the hockey fever at school, but my gender and low social standing kept me on the periphery.

One of the reasons I was an outcast was that my family did not eat Jell-O. Can you believe it? The reason Jell-O was the desired dessert was that inside each box, there was a special hockey coin. My mother thought that Jell-O was a plebeian food, and it was never going to rest on our kitchen shelves, so we couldn't get the round plastic coins that were the team's color and had the player on one side and the team's logo on the other. The kids whose families ate Jell-O and were able to get these plastic coins played a game at recess that they called "pucks." Kids skipped their coins toward the school wall, and whoever's coin got closest to the wall won all the coins in the toss. Gordy Howe and Frank Mahovlich were some big players that kids tossed their coins for. I stood in envy and watched as they played the game and raked in their winnings.

For a girl, I knew a lot about hockey. I gleaned my information from my brothers and the neighborhood boys, and I played the game at the neighborhood rink with boys from all over.

The outdoor rink was actually in the neighbor's backyard. The man had a huge vegetable garden in the summer from which we stole green beans, peas, and carrots. Sometimes, the neighbor lady would give us small Dixie cups filled with sugar. Then we would pull out a stalk of rhubarb from the large-leafed plant. We would then break the leaf off, lick the end of the stalk, and stick it into the sugar. This process rendered the rhubarb sweet enough to eat; it was a very special treat.

But that was the summer, the time when there was no hockey.

Our neighbor constructed the rink by securing long boards to frame the large rectangle for the ice to fill. Then he painstakingly went out for many days in a row and sprayed water into the rectangle. He was a master at this. The ice was always smooth and flat, no holes or bumps—perfect for an afterschool skate. One year he put up flood lights so we could skate at night under the stars.

In Canada, children learn to ice skate at a young age. I was no exception. I vaguely remember using an old rickety chair for stability as I learned to skate, wobbly at first and then without assistance when I was four years old. I could skate backward by age six. I never took a lesson, but I was a strong, confident skater. As was the expectation for girls at the time, I wore figure skates with the toe picks at the front. Girls were supposed to skate like ballerinas on these skates. I preferred to skate as fast as I could, forward and backward.

When I was in grade three, I was finally allowed to join in the hockey skirmish with the neighborhood boys. I endured taunts such as "She skates like a girl," or "What are those little spikes on the front of your skates for?" But I could skate fast, and I could skate backwards, so I didn't care what they said. I was playing hockey.

On the ice, no one passed to me until one day, I pushed my way in, got the puck, and skated fast into a breakaway. To the astonishment of my teammates, I scored a goal. Of course, they called it lucky, but I knew I had done well and had moved up a notch in their estimation of me as a hockey player.

At school, things were still the same. I remained the outsider, watching as kids gambled their skipping skills, risking their precious coins playing pucks. None of my fellow hockey players acknowledged me anywhere but on the rink.

Saturdays were dedicated to hockey in the neighbor's yard. Teams from other neighborhoods were coming over, and we were approaching league status. The neighbor was a teacher who served both as our coach and our referee.

I got to play every game with my team and was a regular scorer. It felt so good to receive a hearty swat on the back from a teammate when I had done well.

One Saturday, we were playing a close game, and the clock was ticking down when one of my teammates yelled to me, "How about one of your breakaways?" With this, I pushed my way to center ice, snuck under the arms of one of the older boys, and stole the puck. I was on my way down the ice towards the goal when the other team came upon me. There must've been at least three. I tried to get out of the triangle of resistance, but my small stature kept me pinned. Whichever way I turned, there was a player from the other team. Trying to be quick, I called to a teammate and sent him the puck. Just as I flicked the puck out of the cluster of players, I felt myself fall forward. To this day, I don't know if I tripped or was pushed. I only know I went down. I went towards the ice, but my head didn't quite make it there. I landed with my eye hitting the cold, hard wooden boards that sided the rink. Working myself to a standing position, I heard a roar of joy, and I knew that my team had scored a goal. I looked down and saw blood on the ice and realized it was dripping from my nose. It was then that I could feel the pain of my injuries. The coach came running up to me, looked at me, and then gathered a big handful of snow and put it to my nose and eye. "We better get you home," he said as he helped me off the ice.

My mother took me in with a thank you to the neighbor and then said to me as the door closed, "That's what you get for playing hockey with those boys! You're just a little girl, you know. Let's look at you." Then she said, "Here, use this to catch the blood." She handed me a dish towel. She put her hand on my forehead and pushed my head back while scrutinizing my injuries. When she touched my nose and eye socket, I screamed in pain, but she said, "I don't think you've broken anything—let's just put some ice on it and give you a couple of aspirin."

So I retired to the den for the rest of the day, watching TV and wishing I was still out playing hockey. By evening, I could see the blue color of a good shiner beginning to show. I had never had a black eye before. I must admit it hurt, but it made me look tough.

The next day was Sunday, and my eye became an increasingly darker blue. Mum didn't want me to go to church looking like that, so I got to stay home with my older sister.

On Monday, when I went to school, all the kids who saw me commented on my black eye. Of course, they all wanted to know how I got it. With great pride, I was able to say, "I got it playing hockey."

That day, one of my teammates gave me a plastic hockey coin at recess. I waited my turn and then joined in the puck's game against the wall. To my surprise, I won all the coins for that toss. I had now joined the pucks players at school. The teammate, who gifted me the coin, said in front of everyone, "She plays pucks as good as she does hockey. And she's got the best black eye I've ever seen."

Uncle Arno's Cabin

My brother, Phil, and I rumbled around in the back seat of our mother's Cadillac. Dust kicked out as we drove along this gravel road. We were headed to our uncle's cottage, but that was all we knew. Uncle Arno was my mother's older brother. He was married to Aunt Marg, and they invited us for a short vacation. Mum had already barked at us to sit down and be quiet, so Phil and I looked out our windows. All there was to see were trees. Where were we going?

We arrived at a boat launch where Uncle Arno stood and waved hello. "Where's your cottage?" I asked.

"Down the river," he said, and pointed to a boat.

"Good lord," said Mum, "we're not going in that, are we?"

"We have to get to the cottage," answered Uncle Arno. "I didn't tell you because I knew you wouldn't come if I did."

"You're right; I wouldn't have. So we can't drive to the cottage then?"

"Nope, it's right on the shore of the Severin River—no roads out that way. Come on, let's get your stuff and get going. Aunt Marg is expecting us. Your car will be safe here."

He gave us all life vests, and we began climbing into the

boat. It was a short, open boat with an outboard motor, nothing fancy. My uncle lifted me in and set me in the middle; he said I weighed no more than a flea.

We bounced along on the water. We saw other buildings at the river's edge—Uncle Arno waved to a few people he saw. Otherwise, none of us talked, least of all Mum. She looked unhappy and stiffly took the bumps as we moved along.

When we arrived at the cottage, Aunt Marg met us at the end of the dock with open arms to welcome us. Phil and I scrambled out as she gave each of us a hug and exclaimed how big we had become. Uncle Arno assisted our mother as she stepped from the boat to the dock.

Aunt Marg said, "Hello Frieda!" and Mum returned her greeting. Uncle Arno grabbed all three suitcases and carried them up to the cottage. Phil and I ran ahead up a hill on a path flanked by wildflowers. Mum took her time getting to the cottage and had to sit down for a rest on a porch chair when she got there. She took her cigarettes from her purse and lit one, then inhaled deeply. My brother and I had already run inside the cabin by this time. It was small with a central kitchen and three doors leading off.

"Come here; I'll show you your room. You two don't mind sharing, do you?" Aunt Marg asked. She opened one of the doors and showed us a room with two narrow beds on each wall, with a small nightstand between them.

"What kind of lamp is that?" I asked Aunt Marg.

"It's a kerosene lantern, dear. We don't have electricity out here, so we use them for light."

"No electricity?" I asked.

"That means no toaster, no television, nothing electric," said Phil.

"I didn't know you could live like that," I said.

"The pioneers did it," replied Phil.

"We do fine," added Aunt Marg.

Aunt Marg left us in our room and fetched our small suitcases for us. I tossed my bag on my bed and headed out to the kitchen, where I heard Mum say, "No electricity? I suppose you don't have water either."

"Oh, no, we have a well with a pump out back." Aunt Marg pointed to the door off the kitchen. "But there's no indoor toilet. We use the kybo out back." Aunt Marg looked at Phil and me. "If you have to go, let us know."

"Now I advise you to wear these when you go out there, 'cause of the snakes," Uncle Arno held up a pair of rubber boots.

"Snakes!" Mum exclaimed. "You can't be serious, Arn."

"Yes I am. There's rattlers around here."

"Now you tell me," Mum said.

"I don't recall you asking."

"Why would I? Really. First, no road, then no lights, now snakes! This is going to be a great five days."

Five days, I thought? Snakes or not, I was thrilled that we got to stay for five whole days. Phil and I tried the boots on. They were tall, past my brother's knees, and they were up to my crotch. Uncle Arno said, "If you need to go at night, come find me even if you have to wake me up. It's pitch black out there. I wouldn't want you to get lost."

To be lost in the woods at night sounded scary to me. I am glad that Uncle Arno said he would take his flashlight with him when he accompanied either of us to the kybo.

Since it was a warm afternoon, Phil and I asked if we could go swimming.

Mum looked at Uncle Arno, "Jennifer can't swim very well. That river is pretty swift."

"Don't worry," he replied, "I've got it all figured out."

Phil and I put our suits on and grabbed a towel. At the dock, I saw that my uncle had two life vests in one hand and some rope in the other. I felt OK about the life vest, so I didn't complain when he told me to put it on. Phil protested a bit, saying that he could swim, but Uncle Arno told him, "There's a mighty strong current in the river." Then, to our surprise, he took one rope and tied it around my waist, and tied the other rope around my brother's waist. The ends of the ropes he fastened to the dock. "Don't want you washing away," he said with a smile.

I wondered what was wrong with washing away. I thought it sounded pretty nice; I loved the book *The Water Babies*, where they'd all washed away.

Phil and I climbed down the ladder and into the water. It was cold, and I could already feel the pull of the river. Uncle Arno took a neat dive off the dock into the water and emerged many feet away. He swam back to us as we floated down the river. When we got to the end of our ropes, we pulled ourselves back to the dock as Uncle Arno swam beside us. He stayed close to us the whole time we were in the water.

When we finally climbed out onto the dock, we shivered and were tired. Uncle Arno untied the rope, removed our life vests, and then gave us a brisk rub down, then wrapped us in our towels. He walked us to the cabin, a hand on each of our shoulders. He told us what good swimmers we were and that we could go swimming again if we wanted.

"Even tomorrow?" I asked.

"Even tomorrow," he answered.

Once back inside the cabin, Aunt Marg announced that dinner would be ready soon, so we'd had better change back into our clothes. "I'm starving," Phil said.

Dinner smelled delicious and looked even more tantalizing. We were each given a plate with a bun, bursting with gooey-looking meat. I waited until Mum led grace before I attempted to pick it up. The flavor was unlike anything I'd ever tasted—nothing like my mother's bland cooking.

"Gee, Aunt Marg this is good. What is it?" I said with my mouth full.

"Sloppy Joes."

I laughed at the funny name. "Well, they taste good to me." I turned toward Mum, "How come you never make Sloppy Joes?" Even the name felt good on my tongue.

Uncle Arno jumped right in and said, "Your Aunt Marg is just a simple cook, nothing fancy like your mum. This here is just out of a can. I bet you never cook with stuff out of a can, eh, Freedy?"

Freedy! Was that Mum's nickname?

Mum made a smug face and shook her head back and forth.

I didn't care. I thought Sloppy Joes were delicious, whether they came from a can or not.

For dessert, we had red gelatin with fake whipped cream. I was happy. Mum told Phil and me to help with the dishes. We were fascinated watching Aunt Marg go outside the back door and pump water into a pot. She had to heat it on the stove to wash the dishes. While we waited, she told us the story about Brer Rabbit. We'd heard it before but kept quiet and let her tell the story. She had a gentle, sweet voice.

After finishing the dishes, Uncle Arno brought out a small suitcase to show Phil and me. When he opened it, we both said together, "Ahhh!" The case was full of dice, game pieces and boards, dominoes, a wheel-type thing, and who knows what else! Uncle Arno said that there were twenty games in the suitcase. He knew how to play most of them, but some he wasn't so sure.

"Don't you have the instructions?" asked Phil.

"No." Uncle Arno shrugged. "They must've been lost a long time ago."

"Oh well," I said, "we can make up the rules if we want."

"Not your rules," said Phil.

As we dove into the games, I heard Mum say to my uncle, "That's an expensive-looking set. Where on earth did you get it?"

"That's my secret, little sister."

We played games until it was time to go to bed. Phil and I hid our eyes while the other got our pajamas on. Aunt Marg came in and gave each of us a kiss. Uncle Arno called, "Good night," at the door. With the lantern blown out, it was very dark. I lay in bed wide awake as I heard Mum's voice swirl with my aunt's and uncle's.

Phil woke me up in the morning when he said, "That sure smells good; it must be breakfast." He left me alone in the room to go out to see. While he was gone, I changed into my clothes. Then joined him.

Aunt Marg was at the stove cooking bacon and pancakes. Phil was right; breakfast smelled delicious. All we ever had at home for breakfast was cereal.

Uncle Arno wished me a good morning, and my aunt kissed me on the top of my head.

I heard the tail end of "…it's a wood stove," from Aunt Marg to Mum.

Uncle Arno said, "There's enough trees around here to keep her cooking for years."

"Huh," Mum said, "suit yourself."

Breakfast was even better than last night's dinner. We never had pancakes with maple syrup at home. Phil and I helped with the dishes again. This time, the water was already hot. When the dishes were done, Uncle Arno asked Phil and me if we wanted to go fishing. "Fishing!" I was so excited.

We both ran to ask Mum. "Of course," she said, but then added, "don't come back with a hook in your finger."

"We won't," I said.

I had never gone fishing before and had no idea what it entailed, but I was game.

We got into his boat, both of us wearing life jackets—Aunt Marg handed down a brown paper bag. Uncle Arno brought a metal box with a handle and two fishing rods. "Only two poles?" Phil asked.

"You two are my fishermen today."

I rather liked the idea of being a fisherman.

We took the boat along the river, letting the current carry us. Uncle Arno guided the boat towards the bank, where the current was slower. He took a heavy brick with a rope on it and threw it overboard as an anchor. "It's not too deep here. Fish like the reeds."

The boat settled into place as he opened his box. Inside were hooks, lures, and a tin with worms in it. I watched as he took a worm and slid it onto a hook. "Doesn't that hurt them?" I asked.

"Nah," he said, "worms don't have brains—you've got to have brains to feel."

"I didn't know that about worms. What about bugs? Can they feel? Do they have brains?" I asked.

"I don't believe they do," Uncle Arno said.

"See, I told you," said Phil, "you can stomp on a bug, and it doesn't feel a thing."

Uncle Arno handed me the fishing pole with the worm on the hook and showed me how to release the line. Then he helped Phil.

With both lines in the water, we sat quietly as the boat rocked in the current.

After a while, Uncle Arno got the brown paper bag that Aunt Marg handed him. "You kids hungry?" he asked.

We positioned our fishing rods against the seat, and then Uncle Arno handed us peanut butter and jelly sandwiches wrapped in waxed paper. There were jam jars full of juice for us to drink, and an apple for later.

While we ate, Phil's reel spun out. He dropped his sandwich and spilled his juice as he grabbed for it. Uncle Arno reached over to help him steady his rod. "Reel it in there, Phil, let's see what you've got. Does it feel big?"

"Huge," yelled Phil, "it's really pulling."

"Take her slow and steady, Phil," Uncle Arno said.

Phil leaned back to reel in the fish, giving it all his

strength. Suddenly, the line went slack, and Phil fell back in the boat.

"Damn," said our uncle, "he must've gotten away. Reel in your line, Phil."

When Phil reeled in his line, there was no hook left.

"Look at that! It must've been a really big one to break the line like that," Uncle Arno said.

We sat in the boat and finished our lunches. Then Uncle Arno said, "Let's go home and tell your mum about the big one that got away."

We bounced around in the boat on the way back. The spray hit our faces.

Mum sat outside reading a book as we arrived home. All she said about Phil's big fish was, "That's nice."

Aunt Marg wanted to hear all about it. She asked how big we thought the fish was, and Phil held his hands at least as wide as his shoulders.

"That big," she said, "oh, my!"

Phil and I spent the next three days swimming and playing games. Sometimes, Uncle Arno even played soccer with us.. Each night, Aunt Marg made another delicious meal for us. And each morning, we were greeted by the tantalizing smell of yet another breakfast cooking.

On our last day, Mum directed us to pack. I shoved my stuff into my bag to make time for another quick round of soccer with my uncle.

Mother announced, "Arn, I'm ready to go now."

"OK, Freedy," he said.

"So soon," said Aunt Marg, and gave Phil and me a big hug and a kiss on the top of the head.

We clamored into the boat and put on our life vests. Mine was still a bit damp from yesterday's swim.

The ride in the boat was bumpy as the spray hit our faces. I looked back as the cottage disappeared from view. Aunt Marg stood on the dock.

When we arrived at the launch, where the car was parked,

Uncle Arno got out first and tied the boat to the dock. He then helped Mum and Phil get out. Me—he picked up, high, gave me a big squeeze and a wet kiss on the cheek before setting me down on the dock. "Goodbye, my little one," he said.

When my feet touched the ground, I felt golden.

A Can Of Dog Food

My mother worked as a teacher when I was growing up. She was not in the house during the day until she got home at about five. I wore a key on a string around my neck so that I could leave school and walk the few blocks home for lunch. I think I was about ten. At lunchtime, I had the house to myself. I enjoyed my time alone with the cat and dog. Sometimes, I would play loud music and dance like a mad fiend, letting my pent-up anger and frustrations out. At other times, I listened to melancholic music while lying on the carpet and cried, releasing my sadness.

Lunch and the subsequent recess were probably an hour. I don't recall being distracted by the time. Sometimes I may have been a few minutes late returning to school, but no one seemed to notice.

This day in spring was like any other. The teacher released us to go to lunch, and I walked home by myself, and used my key to let myself into the house. It was a rare event to be alone in the house. First, I let Daisy, our dog, out so she could do her thing. Then I found Ping, the cat, and patted him. The refrigerator held peanut butter and jelly for my sandwich. The bread was on the counter. I sat down at the table with a glass of milk and ate. My dog came by for a scratch. Daisy was my responsibility. I was supposed to feed her and take her for walks. At my lunch break, I let her out to relieve herself. I would take her for a walk after school. Today, while I was eating, she looked longingly at her dish and then at me. She did this numerous times. There was no food left in it. Usually, there were a few kibbles or a smear of canned food, but today I saw nothing. Oh no, had I forgotten to feed Daisy that day? Maybe that's what she was trying to tell me.

I cleared up my dishes and got her bowl. I put a cup of kibbles in it and opened a can of dog food. The can opener did not slice the top of the can off neatly. The lid hung on to a little piece of metal that I had to work around. In scraping out a few spoon fulls of canned dog food, I caught my right index finger on the sharp lid, and immediately, copious amounts of blood began to flow. I grabbed a napkin from the counter and wrapped it around my finger, which was quickly soaked with blood. I took another napkin and did the same thing. Meanwhile, Daisy waited patiently for her food. I put her bowl on the floor dripping blood on it. I got the dishcloth from the sink and wiped up the blood.

My finger continued to bleed. I wrapped another napkin around it tightly and went to look for a band-aid. As I walked to the bathroom, I dripped blood on the floor. I could only find small band aids for small cuts. This cut was big and still bleeding. I couldn't find any gauze, so I had to use a napkin instead. The bleeding was starting to slow down. I went back into the kitchen, replaced the bloody napkin on my finger with one that I had folded in half, then wrapped it tightly around my finger, and taped it up with Scotch tape. It seemed like the bleeding had stopped. I was relieved. I put my blood-soaked napkins in the garbage and walked back to school.

The playground was empty, which meant that the kids had gone in from recess.

I went into my classroom and sat at my desk. All my classmates were quietly working. I whispered to the girl beside me to find out what they were doing. "Writing," she said as she pointed to the board where the teacher had written, "What does springtime mean to you?" Springtime, I loved it with all the flowers and new life, like the baby bunnies in the field behind the school and the baby birds in the trees. I could write reams about springtime. I got out a pencil and paper and began to write. Crooking my right index finger to hold a pencil caused it to bleed again. I could see the blood soaking the napkin taped to it. It soaked through and began to drip on the paper. I raised my left hand and asked if I could get a tissue. "Go ahead," said my teacher. The tissue box was on her desk, so I had to walk past several of my classmates to reach it. I grabbed a bunch since now the blood was beginning to drip again.

As I walked back to my seat, one of the kids said, "Eeeeyew, gross."

Now that had my teacher's attention, and she came to see what was going on. When she saw the blood, she said, "Jennifer, go to the office right now."

I walked down the long hall to the office, still attempting to quell the flow of blood from my finger.

In the office, I showed the secretary my dilemma, and she said, "Too bad the nurse isn't here today," as she looked at the bloody tissue on my finger. She took me into the sick room and held my hand over the sink. When she removed the tissue, my homemade band-aid of tape and napkin, she could see that it was a sizable cut, maybe an inch and a half in length. "How did you do this?"

"On a can of dog food," I answered.

"Why didn't your mother fix it for you?"

"Because she wasn't home," I answered.

"Where is she?"

"She works," I said.

"I see," said the secretary, "And you're left on your own?"

"I have a key." I pulled out my key on a string from the neck of my blouse.

"Mr. Loftus," the secretary called to the principal, "have a look at this."

Mr. Loftus came in to survey my finger. "It looks like it could use a stitch, I'll have to call her mother," he said and then went back to his office.

"Please don't call my mother," I said.

"Why not?" asked the secretary.

"Because she'll get really mad at me," I said.

"Why is that?"

"She doesn't like to be disturbed, she won't come anyway, she's teaching. Can't you just bandage it up?"

"Alright, I won't call her. I'll wrap it up tight for you—that should stop the bleeding."

First, she ran some water over it, and then she wrapped my finger in a big sausage-sized gauze bandage, and sent me back to class.

By the time I returned to class, we were no longer writing; we had moved onto history. The teacher was at the front of the class, talking about General Brock from the War of 1812 and how there was a monument to Brock in Queenston Heights near Niagara Falls. I zoned out as my finger began to hurt because it was wrapped so tightly. I made a point of not using my finger the rest of the school day.

When school was out, I went home and let myself in. There would be a couple of hours before my mum came home.

I took the dog for a quick walk around the block and then sat in my bedroom and read. I could hear Mum downstairs.

Then I heard the phone ring and I overheard the conversation. "Hello, Mr. Loftus, what has Jennifer done today?"After a long pause, Mum said, "Cut her finger? On a dog food can. Alright, thank you," and she hung up the phone.

She came into my room and said, "Let me see that finger."

When I stuck it out, she grabbed it, which hurt like hell. "What were you doing feeding the dog anyway?"

"It didn't look like she'd been fed," I answered.

"Well, thanks to you, I have to go and meet with Mr. Loftus tomorrow. As if I don't have enough to do." She eyed my finger again, "We'll leave it wrapped up. Don't get it wet."

At dinner time, I tried not to use my finger to eat.

"Oh, just use it! It can't be that bad," Mum said.

"It hurts," I answered, "plus, I'm afraid it might bleed again." I didn't use my finger for the rest of the meal.

I went to school the next day with the same gauzy bandage on. I learned to write with my middle finger and thumb.

That night, my mother said to me, "I bought some band aids for your finger. Take off that big thing and put a new one on it."

I went into the bathroom and removed the old bandage. The cut was crusted with blood, and the skin looked a bit blue. It took three band-aids to cover the wound. My finger felt very vulnerable with just the three band aids on it. I ate my dinner using my thumb and third finger to hold my utensil.

Later that night, Mum got another call from Mr. Loftus. "Hello, Mr. Loftus," I heard her say. After a minute or two, she responded, "The earliest I can be there is four-thirty," then she hung up the phone.

The next day, Mum arrived home later than usual. "I had a talk with Mr. Loftus," she said as a greeting to me. "I thought you were old enough to be on your own at lunch, but I guess not. You're going to have to stay at school from now on. Carrie will make your lunch for you. You are not to come home until after school is out. Do you hear me?"

"Yes, "I said.

"Daisy will be left in the basement, and you will be responsible for cleaning up any messes that she makes. "Do you understand?" Mum continued.

Gone were my times alone in the house, the music, the frenetic dancing, and the cathartic tears. I had to stay at school with all my classmates and eat lunch in the classroom, then go out for recess—just like everybody else. I lost my privilege of solitude all because of a can of dog food.

The Classroom Contest

For some odd reason, our teacher, Miss Hunt seemed to think that hygiene was a subject she should impress upon our young, developing minds. Her lectures about the use of deodorant, wearing clean clothes, refraining from picking our noses, and hand washing were embedded in the typical curriculum of math, history, writing, reading, and the social sciences.

"Now, class, the pioneers may not have had running water, but we do. You all need to bathe and use deodorant regularly now that you're eleven years old," or, "You can do your math facts in your head, as you wash your hands. If you do the times tables up to nine, while you scrub, your hands will be good and clean." If Miss Hunt caught us picking our noses, she would make us go to the bathroom and wash our hands to the count of one-thousand. If we came back to class and our hands weren't obviously red from excessive scrubbing, she would send us back to perform the task again.

She, herself, was respectable-looking. Each day, Miss Hunt wore a neat two-piece suit of a solid color, with a crisp white blouse under the jacket. Her shoes were low heels and sling-backs in the warmer months. She always wore nylons, never bare legs, even when the temperatures reached eighty degrees in late June.

Since this was a Catholic school, we all wore uniforms. The boys wore blue shirts and gray pants, and the girls wore a navy gabardine tunic with a white blouse underneath. I had one tunic and two white blouses. My blouses were washed every weekend, but Mum probably dry-cleaned the tunic two or three times a school year. I don't think Miss Hunt would've approved.

One of my classmates, Mary Hannegan, had several tunics (I could tell because the buttons were different) that she wore with a fresh, clean blouse each day. Once in a while, she wore a dress to school, explaining that all of her tunics were in the dry cleaners. Her dresses were always frilly in various pastel colors, even in the winter. I don't think she ever wore the same outfit twice.

She was an only child, and her parents doted on her. Her long curly hair was always clean and styled with barrettes and ribbons. My hair was long and straight and dishwater blond. Each morning, one of my sisters would brush it out and pull it into a tight ponytail. A ritual I hated since they seemed to enjoy my protests as they tugged on my hair.

Mary would whisper about me behind my back, about how all my clothes were hand-me-downs since I was the youngest of six. And that my socks and panties just came from a big pile in the laundry room. How she knew this fact, I'll never know.

However, I did have one up on her. I was smart: I could recite the catechism verses to perfection; I could do math in my head, and I was the first to answer history facts and could read way beyond my grade level. The only subject I was poor in was penmanship.

One day in January, Miss Hunt announced that there was going to be a contest in class to see who could have the nicest fingernails. She had seen several of us biting our nails. A nasty habit, she said, that not only looked terrible but spread germs, as well. Starting that day, we had two weeks in which to grow our nails and shape them into nice round tips with an emery board. The prize was to be a book chosen by the winning child from the book club to which our classroom subscribed. She walked around the room row by row and showed us her hands, explaining how, on each day, she cleaned underneath her nails and then filed them to keep them neat. Mary raised her hand and said, "My mother paints her nails."

"That's for other women, but not for me," was Miss Hunt's response.

My heart sank as I looked down at my own nails bitten to the quick and hangnails picked to the point of bleeding. Two weeks was not long enough for my nails to grow out. I had probably been chewing my nails since I first got teeth. It was a habit so ingrained in me that I had found my fingers in my mouth upon waking many mornings, and a mixture of saliva and blood dripped out of the side of my mouth onto my pillow. But I also loved to read, and oh, to get a brand new book from the book club would be quite a treat for me. Mum never bought me any books from the book club because she said we had enough at home, and there was also the library. I thought a book from the Nancy Drew series sounded like fun. In our house, we had only books Mum considered to be literature. Titles such as *The Yearling*, *Robinson Crusoe*, and *The Wind in the Willows* donned our shelves. Mum said that the Nancy Drew series was common and not well written.

I thought about my fingernails and how I could break myself of the habit of chewing them. It was so automatic that I didn't even really notice what I was doing unless I got to where it hurt. That might make me pull that finger out of my mouth, but then I still had nine more to chew.

My first idea was to wear gloves. I had a pair of white gloves that I wore to church in the warm months. They were light. Surely I could write and use my hands for other tasks while protecting my fingernails from being chewed.

I snuck my gloves into my pocket because I knew full and well that Mum would disapprove of me taking my good gloves to school.

When I got to school, I put my gloves on and sat at my desk. "What have you got on your hands?" my neighbor whispered to me.

"Gloves," I whispered back and then pretended to bite my nails and shook my head.

"Good idea," my friend said back to me.

I managed to keep my gloves on most of the morning without any repercussions, until our writing time. Then, when I got out my fountain pen and my notebook, Miss Hunt was by my side.

"Jennifer, while I admire your conviction to try to stop chewing your nails, you cannot wear gloves for penmanship. Your writing is illegible enough without the impediment that gloves would give you." She held out her hand. I removed the gloves and gave them to her. Would she give them back to me?

As I did our assignment I forgot about the contest. I put my index finger of my left hand into my mouth and nibbled away. Before long, I had chewed every fingernail of my left hand. There were a few smears of ink on the left side of my paper as I tried my best to write legibly.

When the end of the school day came, I asked for my gloves. Miss Hunt said, "Jennifer, it may be impossible to bite your nails with gloves on, but gloves aren't practical at school. Please leave them at home. What you need to do is be strong and say to yourself, ' I must not bite my nails, I must not bite my nails.'"

That night, I went into the medicine cabinet and got out the box of band aids. Before I left for school the next day, I put a band aid on the end of each finger.

This worked very well until Mary Hannegan tattled on me during math. "Jennifer was picking her nose, I saw her."

Miss Hunt sent me to the washroom to keep scrubbing my hands until I had counted from one to one-thousand. During the rigorous scrubbing, many of the slim bandages came off my fingertips. By the end of the day, I was back to chewing my fingernails again.

At home that night, I asked my favorite sister what she thought might help. She said she'd heard that to get a little kid to stop sucking their thumb, people put yucky-tasting stuff on it.

"Like what I asked?"

"Mustard, horseradish, vinegar. I'm not sure, but you could try that."

The next day, I got the jar of mustard out of the fridge and stuck it into my pocket before school. At school, I put the jar in my desk and took the lid off. I carefully dipped each fingertip into the mustard and went about my school day.

The girl sitting in front of me asked what the smell was, and I told her, "Turn around, it's nothing."

The first subject was math, and I was able to keep my fingers out of my mouth the whole time. Maybe this was going to work. Then we had silent reading. I was deep into *Beautiful Joe*, a book I had gotten from the school library about an abused dog that gets rescued by a kind girl. I was so engrossed in the book that I found myself mindlessly chewing past the mustard to my fingernails. Maybe mustard wasn't a bad enough flavor for me.

The next day, I tried horseradish. I knew I didn't like the taste of this. In fact, I thought it was horrid. The jar was only about a third full, but I was certain that even the smallest amount of the wretched-tasting stuff could keep me from chewing my fingernails.

When I opened the jar of horseradish at my desk, no one said a thing. I dabbed some horseradish on the tip of each finger. I could feel it sting on the raw flesh of my chewed-up fingertips. It didn't stick very well, and some slid off onto the floor. Several kids around me made comments: "EEYYOO, what's that stink?"

"Smells like someone's dirty feet."

Miss Hunt was at my desk within seconds. "Jennifer, what have you got in your desk?"

I looked up at her but didn't want to respond, so I just played dumb. One of the kids pointed to the white glob on the floor and said, "It looks like bird poop."

Miss Hunt told me to stand beside my desk while she bent over to look inside it. There she found the jar of horse-radish.

"Jennifer, what is this?"

"Horseradish sauce," I said.

"And why do you have horseradish sauce in your desk?"

"Because I like it?" I said.

"You like it, do you?" Miss Hunt said.

"Uh huh."

"I don't believe you," she said, "show me, eat some."

I put my finger into the jar and pulled out a small glob.

"More than that," she said.

I put my finger back into the jar and fished out as big a glob as I could hold on my finger.

All the kids around me were going, "EEYYOO."

The whole class looked at me. I put the glob of horseradish into my mouth, and immediately my eyes started to water. I thought I was going to vomit. But I wasn't going to let Miss Hunt and the whole class have the privilege of seeing me get sick. Instead, I quickly swallowed the glob and smiled the best smile I could muster. "Mmmm," I said.

"Jennifer, I do not want to see that horseradish or any other food items in your desk. Do you hear me?"

Totally humiliated, I had to go through the rest of the day with neighs and horse snorts directed at me from my classmates.

At home that night, I talked with my sister again. She asked me, "Why do you bite your fingernails anyway?"

"I don't know, it's just a habit, I guess."

"How about a new habit?" she asked.

"Like what?"

"How about a bracelet to twirl on your wrist or a ring to wear on your finger?"

"How about both?" I asked her.

I went to school the next day wearing my sister's charm bracelet and her birthstone ring. During math, I fidgeted with the jewelry and kept my fingers out of my mouth. During reading, I twirled the ring and read *Beautiful Joe*. During writing, I felt the bracelet clinking on my desk as I completed my assignment. It worked; I was set. I could feel my fingernails growing.

That night at home, Mum noticed the jewelry. "Why are you wearing your sister's good jewelry?" To my sister, she said, "Why did you loan Jennifer your jewelry?"

Then the whole story about the fingernail contest at school came out. I even included the gloves, the horseradish, and the humiliation of it all. Mum listened for a while and then she went to her purse. She took out her checkbook and wrote a check for one-hundred dollars with my name on it. Then she said, "Jennifer, if you can stop chewing your nails in a month, you can have this check."

I couldn't believe it. My mother, the tightwad, just offered me a hundred dollars to stop chewing my nails. That was way more than Miss Hunt had to offer. I could buy a whole bunch of books with that money. I could buy myself some clothes. I could even go to a movie. I could maybe buy those beautiful ice skates that I really wanted for Christmas and my birthday, but didn't get. I'd be rich. I could do it. I could stop chewing my nails.

In a month, Mum and I sat down at the kitchen table. "OK, let's see those nails," she said to me. I held out my hands, and there at the tips were small crescent nails and intact skin. I had given up chewing my nails for good. She handed me the check, and the next day we went to the bank where I cashed it.

As for the classroom contest, of course, Mary Hannegan won. I felt sick to my stomach as she told the class how she cleaned her nails each day with a nail brush and filed them just a little bit to keep them in good shape. Before Mary took her seat, she looked right at me, and I stuck out my tongue. She sat down, raised her hand, and said, "Jennifer just stuck her tongue out at me."

The Rescue

History has never been much of an interest to me, and in grade four it was even less so. Miss Hunt, our teacher, struck me as very detached and seemed to lack any enthusiasm for her job.

We all had our textbooks out. The cover portrayed a soldier in full English red regalia. There was water in the background and a ship on the horizon. The title of the book was *The Second World War.* The war had been a reality for my parents, and two of my sisters were born during that time. My dad, as a doctor, was never called to duty but had to be at the ready. Oftentimes, I heard the war referred to during conversation in our house, even when our dad no longer lived with us.

Miss Hunt had just reviewed what we had studied the previous day. Canada had ships called corvettes that patrolled the west coast of Europe and England on the lookout for German submarines. We left off the day before at the part where the Canadian ships had sailed into dangerous territory.

"Who would like to read?" Miss Hunt asked. No one raised their hand. "Very well then, Michael, stand up and read for us."

Michael, was Michael McSorley, at least that's what we always called him. He was a rather short, chubby, and always well-groomed classmate. He wore wool vests and long-sleeved plaid shirts that looked as if someone had ironed them. Probably his loving mother. His hair was in a brush cut, and so short at the back of his neck that his skin showed through. Due to his extra weight, he had a fold of skin at the back of his neck that pushed a little bit over the collar of his shirt. Michael was not a popular kid; he lacked the ability to let go and be silly, always serious. He never joined in with the sports at recess. However, he seemed to have a few friends he hung out with, so in my young eyes, he wasn't a total loss.

Michael stepped out into the aisle next to his desk, book splayed open in his hands in front of him.

He cleared his throat and began reading.

About this time, I slid into my own little world of playing in the woods, jumping rope, or roller skating, anything fun but, definitely, not history. Then I heard a word that sounded out of sync with the material that Michael was reading. I heard him say, "Sauce, *Sauce!*" With some enthusiasm.

Sauce? Why would a history book have the word sauce in it? I peered into the text and looked along the page that Michael was reading. It was "S.O.S.," a call from a ship. "Save Our Ship." Clearly, the Canadian ship was in trouble. Again, he said, "Sauce! Sauce!"

Now, my fellow classmates were looking at one another, tittering at Michael as he read. He obviously did not know what he was reading. He was not aware of his error. By this time, he had said so many "sauces" that he was spitting slightly, and his classmates were now outwardly laughing at him. He had turned a bright red. Poor Michael.

I looked at Miss Hunt, and she seemed to be asleep. If not that, then at least daydreaming.

I couldn't stand it any longer. I raised my hand and said loud enough to draw her from her reverie, "Miss Hunt, Michael could use some help!"

"How so?" she asked.

I decided to take matters into my own hands, and I said directly to Michael McSorley, "It's S.O.S. Save our Ship, the ship is in trouble. It could also be Save our Souls."

Michael looked at me and burst into tears, sputtering and sniffling. The rest of the class remained quiet. He sat down at his desk and put his head in his hands.

Miss Hunt said, "Thank you, Jennifer, for rescuing Michael. He seems to lack an understanding of the Morse Code signal for distress."

Our class was collectively relieved when the bell soon rang at the end of the school day.

Miss Hunt said, "Class dismissed," and we gathered our things to wait at the door for the final dismissal. Michael remained in his seat. I went up to him and said, "I'm sorry, Michael, I just had to say something."

"I feel like such a fool," he said.

"Don't worry, it will all be forgotten," I said as he got out of his seat.

"You rescued me," he said. "Thanks"

***

All has not been forgotten. I remember this incident clearly, and I wonder how many of my other classmates have held this humiliating event in their memories, even though it was over sixty years ago. I wish him well.

My First Kiss

Summer camp was my welcome respite from my everyday life growing up. My older sister, brother, and I left for camp a few days after school was out and returned home just before school started. A whole two months away from home. The year I turned thirteen, Mum told us that this would be our last summer at camp.

As the youngest of six, the camp offered a release from the tension of my home life with my depressed and volatile mother and a deferment from the social oppression I felt at school. My life felt like a barren wasteland of rules, expectations, and religious authority. I lived on the periphery of the social culture of my school. I had few friends and was not allowed any extracurricular activities that, no doubt, I would have loved. My life consisted of the rigidity of Catholic school and the dysfunction of my unaffectionate home environment. I spent numerous hours in my room alone. The chaos of my family life gave me little opportunity to feel secure within myself.

Camp, however, felt cozy and nurturing. The staff and my fellow campers liked me. I felt cared for. Our accommodations were large canvas tents on wooden platforms. Six girls slept in a bunk bed setup. We had no electricity; we relied only on the light of our flashlights. I was lulled into sleep each night by the sounds of nature. We had an outhouse, or kybo, as it was called in Canada, and bathed in Big Hawk Lake, at our doorstep. We ate as a whole camp: boys, girls, and staff in a log cabin lodge. Our counselor was a teenager, full of fun and hugs. I loved her.

For meals, we sat in tent groups with our counselor. At breakfast, announcements were made regarding any schedule changes due to weather or otherwise, as well as birthdays and celebrations. At lunch, the tent inspection results were given. Based on a ten-point scale, the tent that got the closest to a score of seventy for the days of the week won a delectable cake with mouthwatering frosting. What a special treat that was—the cake was large enough to feed twenty. When our tent won in the first week of camp, our counselor asked if we would like to share the cake with the boys' tent, campers our age.

Six thirteen-year-old boys joined us. I could tell by their interactions that our counselors were well acquainted. The girls sat on one side of the table and the boys on the other. Before the counselors served the cake, they asked us to state our name, where we came from, and maybe a little about ourselves. I paid little attention to the boys as they recited their names and home until the boy across from me, Angus McTavish, said he was from Ottawa and attended the elite boys' school called Auburn. He looked right at me with his deep blue eyes, his nose dotted with freckles, and black, slightly curly hair. I averted my eyes as I felt shy under his gaze. I felt an unfamiliar stirring in my stomach.

"That's a cute swimsuit," said my tentmate, Lorrie, between bites of cake.

Unaccustomed to compliments, I looked down at my blue and white ruffled two-piece and said, "Yeah, I had to talk my mother into buying this for me." Lorrie's swimsuit was a plain navy blue tank suit.

Maybe because we were the same age, the girls began swimming lessons and canoeing with the boys with whom we shared the cake. One day, Angus looked appreciatively at my two-piece suit and said, "You look cute." I had never been called cute by a boy before and had no idea how to respond. I merely smiled at him, and he reached for me and touched my arm when he smiled back.

From then on, I noticed Angus watching me. He was even bold enough to invite me to go canoeing with him. My life vest embarrassed me, although it was customary, even if Angus didn't have to wear one. As the steersman, he made the rules. Our only conversation consisted of him asking me to use a specific stroke. "Jennifer, front right rudder, please." We paddled along the coast of the lake. At one point, we steered into the rushes along the shore. In a whisper, he said, "Look to the left, a bittern,"

I saw a bird as large as a duck in a nest of sticks and leaves among the rushes. I assumed it was the mother bittern with her head raised straight above her body, her yellow eyes watching us. "She does that as camouflage," Angus told me, "to blend into her surroundings."As we pulled the canoe out of the water, he said, "That was special,"

"What was?" I asked

"To see a bittern on her nest."

"I thought it was unusual,"

"They are related to herons, only they're smaller. I'm going to be sure to tell the guys."

As with breakfast and lunch, the camp leader announced the evening's activities at dinnertime. Activities included singing in the dining hall, which we did each night, and sometimes archery, an evening canoe ride, a sail, or a campfire on the beach. The camp leader also used this time to share special happenings from that day's activities. On the evening of my canoe ride with Angus, I was surprised to hear, "Angus and his friend had a rare sighting today. Come on up, Angus, and tell us what you saw."

Angus came over to my table. "Come on," he said to me, "you were there too," and took me by the elbow to the front of the dining hall.

We stood side by side in front of the camp, including my older sister and brother. "Today over in the rushes on the east side of the lake, Jennifer and I saw a mother bittern on her nest."

"That's a very special sighting," said the camp leader. "How big was it?"

"Show 'em, Jennifer," Angus said.

Relieved to not have to talk, I held one hand by my forehead and the other by my waist. Comments of "Wow," and "That's neat," were heard amongst those in the dining hall.

As the weeks went by, Angus and I became good friends. We often went canoing together. We enjoyed archery and hiking. Conversation with him was easy once I got over my shyness. It was obvious that his family had money. All the clothes he wore were new and stylish. He had many pairs of shoes and several jackets. He had a sweatshirt and a t-shirt from his school, Auburn. Except for my new swimsuit and windbreaker, I wore hand-me-downs from my older sister. Angus still told me I looked cute even if I wore my sister's old clothing. I had one pair of flip-flops and one pair of tennis shoes, and that was all. If he attended my high school, I knew he would be one of the cool kids while I hid in the shadows, too self-conscious to be noticed by such a popular guy. I knew his attraction to me was a camp thing, which was OK with me.

We called candy and small merchandise "tuck," and a small shop off the dining hall sold it. The shop kept track of our purchases, and our parents paid for the extras after camp was over. I bought some tuck in my first year at camp, and my mother got very mad at me, saying she didn't have the money to buy me candy. I didn't visit the tuck shop after that.

After lunch one day, Angus asked, "You want some tuck? On me?"

I was pleased.

Angus and I stood at the tuck window. "What do you like?" he asked.

"I don't know. What about MacIntosh's Toffee,"

"Hey, I like that, too. Let's get one?"

The person at the tuck shop knew Angus, so he added the candy to his bill. We took the red package of toffee and sat on the steps of the lodge to enjoy it. When Angus took the hard candy and banged it on the step, my heart leaped up, for that was exactly how I broke the candy into pieces. He pulled the waxed paper out of the box and put it on the step between us. "Help yourself," he said as he motioned towards the candy. The first piece tasted buttery sweet. We sat on the steps and enjoyed the toffee together. He was a nice guy.

One morning after breakfast, on our way to our activities, Angus stopped me and said, "Here, I made this for you." He pulled out a plastic lace bracelet and said, "It's blue and white like your swimsuit." He put it over my hand, but it was too large for my wrist. "I guess I made it too big. I didn't realize how petite you were. I'll fix it."

"Thanks anyway." No one had ever made anything for me before. I felt special.

That evening, as the fire burned to coals and dusk was upon us, a tall man named Tom stood up. He had a blanket shrouded over his head and shoulders while he held a flashlight under his chin to shine on his face. The effect created dark shadows around his eyes while illuminating his face. He then sang a song he called "Riggedy Tiggedy Tin." The song was about a crazy young woman and how she killed each of her family members. I remember the "Riggedy Tiggedy Tin" song, especially the chorus, "…one day when she had nothing to do, she cut her baby brother in two, and put him in an Irish stew and invited the neighbors in." The song gave me the shivers. Then Tom told a story about the creature of Big Hawk Lake, "neither man nor beast," swam through the waters. Tom said the creature once tipped a canoe and pulled the paddlers down to the depths of the water. The creature was known to come out of the lake at night and walk amongst the tents and buildings of the campground. I started to tremble in fear.

Angus whispered in my ear, "It's only a story. It's not true. I'll walk you back tonight." I already felt better. We walked hand-in-hand toward my tent. My counselor met us at the beginning of the girls' section and said, "That's good, Angus. I'll take her from here." Angus squeezed my hand and said goodnight.

I fell asleep that night with warm feelings about Angus. I also experienced a shade of aversion and fear from Tom's song and story, which were the finale to the campfire.

After breakfast, Angus found me the following day and said, " I meant to tell you last night, but I forgot. I'll be gone for five days."

"Where're you going?"

"On a canoe trip."

"Where to?" I asked.

"Clear Lake."

"That sounds fun. I love canoe trips, but ours only lasted three days. It was great. I'm sure you'll have fun. But I'll miss you."

"I'll miss you too." And he smiled at me.

I was swimming as I watched his group of four canoes paddle across the lake and disappear into the forest beyond.

The five days passed quickly enough, but I missed Angus. When the day came for the boys to return, the whole camp watched the lake to catch a glimpse of the canoes coming across. Then they were there. We saw them paddle in unison like a respectable troop. I could feel the excitement in my chest as they approached. Soon, I picked out Angus, the steersman of the second canoe. I stood on my tippy toes and waved high with both my arms. He lifted his paddle in acknowledgment.

When the four canoes pulled onto the shore of Big Hawk Lake, I was right there to greet them. I watched as they laid their paddles across the gunwales. Angus had a big smile on his face as he stepped out into the water. I ran to him. He put his arms around me, and we hugged until his counselor said, "That's enough of that." I was surprised at how soft and warm his body felt and how he smelled like sweat. I wasn't used to being hugged, especially by a boy.

I stood near him as he told about campfires, skinny-dipping, and traversing the land to a logging mill. He said he had a great time, but he was tired. They had to get their gear and put the canoes away.

That night, after dinner, Angus and I went to the dock and sat with our feet dangling into the water. We heard a loon's call echo across the lake. "We have only three weeks left of camp, you know," he said.

"Only three weeks?" I already felt myself missing him all over again. I knew that when we parted on the last day, we would return to our former lives. There was never any talk of keeping in touch.

The camp buzzed about the musical, *The Wizard of Oz,* which we would perform on the last night of camp. Everyone got an assignment. Some campers were responsible for the set, and some created the costumes. We had a line coach, and one of the counselors would accompany us on piano. The youngest campers were assigned the roles of Munchkins, and one of the oldest girls was cast as Dorothy. An older boy got to be the Wizard, and the Wicked Witch was to be played by another older girl. I got the part of the Scarecrow, and Angus was the Tin Man. One of his friends was the Cowardly Lion. Our coach gave us our lines with the directive that we should have them memorized by the last night. At first, this seemed daunting since we had only ten days left of camp.

I carried my page of lines with me all day, and any chance I had to practice, I would, albeit quietly and to myself. I was thrilled to have a singing part, since the nun at Catholic school told me I couldn't carry a tune. Whenever we had a choir concert, I was relegated to the top level at the far end, almost behind the curtain. I always knew the lines, but the choir teacher told me not to sing loudly. Now, I had a chance to shine.

Angus and I were out canoing one day, and he began to sing his Tin Man song. "When a man's an empty kettle, and he should be on his mettle, And yet I'm torn apart," his voice was strong and midrange. He fumbled with the words, and finally, I asked, "Do you have your sheet with you?'

He went to the pocket of his shorts and pulled out his lines neatly folded. I lay my paddle across the thwarts, turned around, and took the page from his hand. "I'll help you."

Together, we were able to get him through the song. Then he said, "How about your lines?"

Pleased as punch, I was able to sing my whole bit. He was quite amazed.

He then began to sing, "Somewhere Over the Rainbow." I joined him, adding bits and pieces of the song. By the third time through, we sang the whole thing. What fun we had!

When we brought the canoe to the shore, my counselor said, "You two sounded pretty good out there." I felt embarrassed because I hadn't realized our voices carried across the water.

At the craft shop, one of the campers on duty made Angus a cone hat and a box to wear on his body. These were painted gray. On the evening of the show, Angus was going to cover his arms with aluminum foil. His Tin Man was looking good.

For my Scarecrow costume, my counselor borrowed a pair of coveralls, and I wore my flannel shirt, which I think had been my brother's, given the backward buttoning of it. My costume person got hay from the bales used for archery and found me a straw hat. I was ready.

All the players rehearsed their parts each day after dinner, and we ran through the whole thing twice. The director said it was only for camp and didn't need to be perfect.

We were all dressed and ready to go on the night of the show. The play took place in the dining hall, with the tables pushed aside and the benches around the room, leaving the end open by the fireplace. We entered and exited by the front door. Excitement buzzed as we waited in the wings for our entrance. Angus needed some help with his lines, but I sang through mine without problems. The Lion wrote his lines on the paper bags that were his paws. We all got a good laugh as he held up the bags to read his lines. The whole thing went off with mistakes, but also lots of laughs.

When the musical was over, we gathered at the front and sang "Somewhere Over the Rainbow" as a whole camp. It was a magical moment.

The counselors served us a huge cake with "Goodbye" written on it—celebrating our success of the musical. Bedtimes were forgotten as we sang and talked into the night. Finally, my counselor took me to my tent. I said goodnight to Angus and left.

The following day was all hustle and bustle as we prepared to leave for home. Some parents picked up their campers. Most went home by bus. My sister, brother, and I would take the bus south to Toronto. Angus would go east to Ottawa.

Those going on buses milled around in the parking lot, waiting to board. Angus approached me and said, "Come here," and motioned me behind the bus. Like a puppy, I followed him. We stood facing each other. Angus took one step towards me, he then put one hand on my back and the other behind my head, tilted his face, and kissed me. The kiss surprised me, but I became appreciative when he kept his lips on mine. When we parted, my mouth felt warm and moist.

"Goodbye, Jennifer. There's my bus," he said as I watched him walk away.

The noise of the ride back and the days at camp drift in my memory, but I will never forget my first kiss.

Thank you, Angus.

Bonus Pages

Jennifer Jamieson Woods' premier novel, *No Guarantees,* takes young Josephine Duckworth from her Oakville, Ontario life, to Anchorage, Alaska, in the 1970s, where young men, hired on to build the Trans-Alaska Pipeline, play as hard as they work. When Josie arrives on vacation at her sister's, her small world enlarges. The freedom from her mother's expectations and rules tantalizes her, and Josie decides to stay. Rod Kohlber, with his Cat Stevens beard and a love of partying, catches her eye, and he's not counting how many gin and tonics she drinks.

No Guarantees is a coming-of-age novel that takes the reader on Josie Duckworth's journey as she negotiates a rock-strewn path to adulthood.

From No Guarantees

Josephine Duckworth liked to consider herself clean and tidy. She felt more at ease when things were spic and span. More than once she had been known to say, "Cleanliness is next to godliness, so please don't be ungodly."

And so it was today, this Saturday as she set about her chores, she wasn't disgruntled about housework; in fact, she rather enjoyed it. She had long ago made friends with the vacuum and the mop, The squeegee she saw as a terrific tool that could lead to sparkling results. All her chores pleased her. She had a lightness of step and a tune in her head as she went about her business. However, she saved her least favorite chore for the last.

She had the task at hand; she had her rubber gloves, her brush, and her economy-sized bottle of Pine-Sol. She was ready to do the dirty job and get it over and done with until next week. There it was in front of her, the porcelain god, the commode, the "terlet," and it needed to be cleaned. She lifted the lid covering the gaping and often foul-smelling hole. The second lid that rings the bowl was the one where she sat her bottom. A woman who lived alone would only need to lift these two lids for the weekly scrub and no other time.

And there it was on the back of the toilet, "Kohler," the blue/black lettering, so close to the name of her first love, a marriage, a relationship that would change her life forever and would always be responsible for whom she became.

Sometimes when she cleaned the toilet, she could glance at the name with no feelings, no remembrances, but today she lingered a bit too long, staring at the letters. Today, she said quietly to herself, "Kohlber, Rod Kohlber."

There she had done it. She had spoken the name aloud. She had taken that extra little step toward her memories, just enough to jar her consciousness to those days when she and Rod were together.

And this is where Josie's story begins ...

ACKNOWLEDGMENTS

These stories tell about my life as a young person. I'd like to acknowledge my sister, Candy, who was always my roommate and gave me lots of grist for the mill. To my sister, Liz, who explained the facts of life to me. To my sister, Wendy, who took me to many dog and cat shows. I can identify lots of dog and cat breeds because of that—a useful skill when walking in the park on a sunny day. My friends are impressed by my knowledge. To my brother, Dave, who ran like the wind in the woods behind our house, and who found raspberry haven, a favourite place to visit in the heat of the summer. To my brother, Tom, with whom I drove all the way to Ottawa in a wintry blizzard to attend Liz's graduation from medical school.

I would be lost if it weren't for Mary Gillillan. She has been my rock throughout my writing career. She always has a way of helping me feel confident and willing to step out and write a book. You are my angel.

Thank you to my friend Christine Griffin for the author portrait and memorable photo of my buddy, Small.

Last but not least, I have tremendous gratitude for my husband, Roger, and my son, Aidan, who have listened to my stories repeatedly. Thank you for your feedback, patience, and unconditional love. You are the best.

ABOUT THE AUTHOR

Wickedly funny and soul-tested, Jennifer Jamieson Woods is delighted to present *Short Shots, Childhood Stories for Grown-up Kids*. Her debut novel, *No Guarantees* spins a yarn of love, loss, and redemption and is available on Amazon or by order from a bookseller close to you.

Born in Canada, Jennifer was the youngest of six children. Her confrontations with Sister Bertrand began at age six, and those memories, like others, are faithfully rendered in *Short Shorts*. The award-winning literary magazine, *Clover, A Literary Rag*, published many of these stories. Jennifer's spare writing style and unerring willingness to consult her angels and her devils shine in her storytelling.

Jennifer retired as a special education teacher and has worked with such organizations as hospice and toddler programs in Bellingham, Washington, where she lives with her husband, Roger. Their lanky red-headed son lives nearby and is a source of continuing joy in her life.

A world traveler, Jennifer gleans material from those she meets on her adventures. Joy is always tempered with the hard-won knowledge that in life there are no guarantees. Let's bless the sunshine and carry on.

www.ingramcontent.com/pod-product-compliance
Lightning Source LLC
Chambersburg PA
CBHW050035040726
47599CB00015B/1689

* 9 7 8 1 7 3 4 1 8 7 8 8 5 *